A Snowman

Written by Rose Kelbrick
Illustrated by Andrea Jaretzki

I have two eyes.

I have two eyes and a mouth.

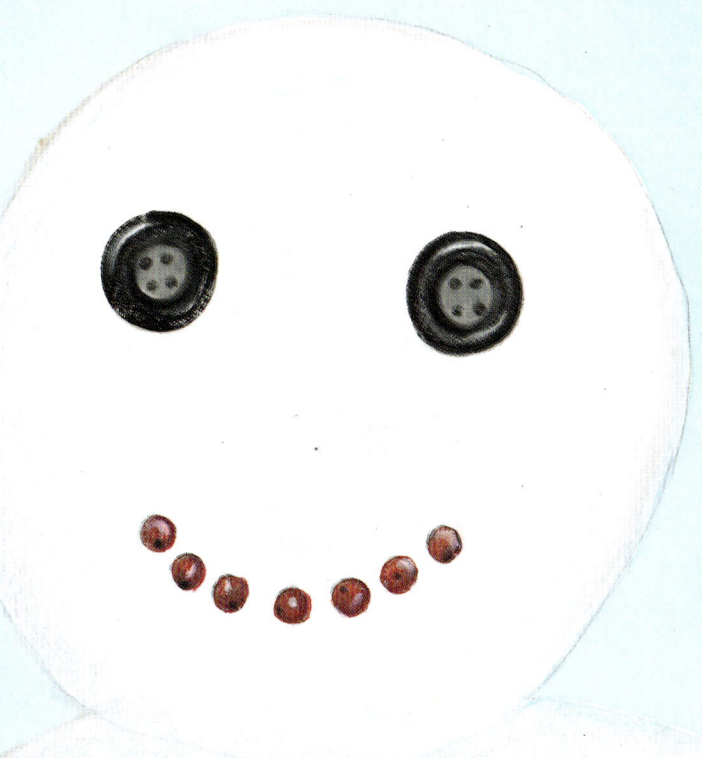

I have two eyes
and a mouth
and a nose.

I have two eyes
and a mouth
and a nose
and a hat.

I have two eyes
and a mouth
and a nose
and a hat
and a scarf.
I am made of snow.

I am a snowman.